I Can't Believe I'm *Quilting*
BEYOND THE BASICS

Dear Reader,
Now that you have learned the basics from my *I Can't Believe I'm Quilting, Beginner's Complete Guide*, I want to introduce you to some advanced quilting techniques that will enhance your skills and spark your creativity.

In this book you will learn my easy method for making Flying Geese, how to speed the quilt making process with Chain Piecing, and the secrets to perfect Curved Piecing. You will experience the fun of Paper-Piecing, give your quilt a different look by setting Blocks on Point, and much more!

Each technique is presented in lesson form with a companion project. The size of the projects — throws, table runners, and wall hangings — allows you enough practice time to get comfortable with your new skills yet still finish the projects quickly.

However, as the photography from my workshop shows, you may choose not to make a whole quilt and just practice the various techniques on sample pieces like my students did.

I wish you the best of luck as you explore this next level of quilting. I know you will use these new skills over and over again when you quilt!

Happy Quilting!

Pat

LEISURE ARTS, INC.
Little Rock, Arkansas

CONTENTS

LESSON ONE

Over the years I have tried many different techniques to make Flying Geese Units. The method I teach in this lesson, **Quick and Easy Flying Geese**, page 6, is the one I like the best. There is very little waste AND you are making 4 Flying Geese Units at a time—what a bonus!

Fly *Away*

My Fly Away quilt makes a striking table runner or wall hanging. I used bold black and white prints with bright red accents, but you can use any color combination you like. So, pick some fabric and let's make a flock of "Geese"!

Finished Quilt Size: 20½" x 37" (52 cm x 94 cm)
Finished Block Size: 6" x 3" (15 cm x 8 cm)

FABRIC REQUIREMENTS

Yardage is based on 43"/44"
(109 cm/112 cm) wide fabric.
- ½ yd (46 cm) of black print
- ½ yd (46 cm) of white print
- ⅜ yd (34 cm) of red tone-on-tone print (includes binding)
- ¾ yd (69 cm) of backing fabric

You will also need:
- 24½" x 41" (62 cm x 104 cm) rectangle of batting

CUTTING OUT THE PIECES

*Follow **Rotary Cutting**, page 54, to cut fabric. Cut all strips from the selvage-to-selvage width of the fabric.*

From black print:
- Cut 2 strips 7¼" wide. From these strips, cut 9 **square A's** 7¼" x 7¼".

From white print:
- Cut 4 strips 3⅞" wide. From these strips, cut 36 **square B's** 3⅞" x 3⅞".

From red tone-on-tone print:
- Cut 2 **sashing strips** 1¼" x 36½".
- Cut 4 **binding strips** 1½" wide.

ASSEMBLING THE QUILT TOP

*Follow **Piecing**, page 54, and **Pressing**, page 55, to assemble the quilt top. Refer to **Quilt Top Diagram** for Unit orientation. Use ¼" seam allowances throughout.*

1. Follow **Quick and Easy Flying Geese**, page 6, to make 36 **Unit 1's**.

Unit 1 (make 36)

TIP: To ensure sharp points when sewing Units together, stitch across the center of the "X" (shown in pink) formed on wrong side by previous seams (**Fig. 1**).

Fig. 1

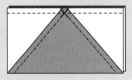

2. Matching right sides and long edges, sew 12 Unit 1's together to make a vertical **Row**. Make 3 vertical rows.

3. Reversing the orientation of the center row, sew 3 rows and 2 **sashing strips** together to make **quilt top**.

Quilt Top Diagram

FINISHING THE QUILT

1. Follow **Quilting**, page 55, to mark, layer, and quilt. My quilt is outline quilted in each of the white triangles. There is a continuous line of meander quilting stitched through the center of the black triangles.

2. Refer to **Making a Hanging Sleeve**, page 58, to make and attach a hanging sleeve, if desired.

3. Use **binding strips** and follow **Pat's Machine-Sewn Binding**, page 58, to bind quilt.

QUICK AND EASY FLYING GEESE

This technique is so much fun that once you have tried it you may never make Flying Geese Units using any other method.

Below I demonstrate making Flying Geese Units using the black large square A's and white small square B's from my Fly Away quilt, page 2.

Note: *I used a high contrast thread for photography purposes only. You will want to use a matching or blending thread when making your project.*

1. Draw a diagonal line on wrong side of each **square B** (**Fig. 1**).

Fig. 1

2. With right sides together, place 1 **square B** on opposite corners of a **square A**; pin in place (**Fig. 2**).

Fig. 2

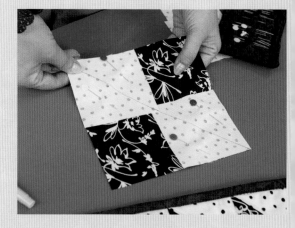

3. Stitch seam ¼" from each side of drawn line (**Figs. 3-4**).

Fig. 3

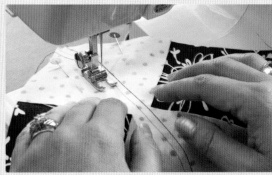

Fig. 4

4. Cut along drawn line (**Fig. 5**). Press seam allowances toward B (**Fig. 6**) to make 2 **Unit 1's**.

Fig. 5

Fig. 6

Unit 1 (make 2)

5. With right sides together, place 1 square B on corner of 1 Unit 1 (**Fig. 7**). Stitch seam ¼" from each side of drawn line (**Fig. 8**).

Fig. 7

Fig. 8

6. Cut along drawn line (**Fig. 9**). Press seam allowances toward B (**Fig. 10**) to make 2 **Flying Geese Units**. Repeat with remaining Unit 1 and another square B to make a total of 4 Flying Geese Units.

Fig. 9

Fig. 10

Flying Geese Unit (make 4)

7. Repeat Steps 1-6 to make the total number of Flying Geese needed. For my Fly Away quilt, that would be a total of 36 Flying Geese Units.

Note: Sometimes, depending on the accuracy of your seam allowances, the Flying Geese Units may need to be trimmed to the exact size. Measure your Units and carefully trim if needed.

DOING THE MATH

For each of the projects in this book the exact cutting sizes and number of pieces to cut for the Flying Geese Units are given to you in the project instructions. However, by following the steps below, you can make Flying Geese Units any size you desire for future projects.

1. To make **4** Flying Geese Units, you will need **1 square A** of fabric for the large center triangle and **4 square B's** of a contrasting fabric for the side triangles. For example, let's say the project calls for 36 Flying Geese Units. You would need 9 square A's (36 ÷ 4 = 9) and 36 square B's.

2. For cutting sizes for squares A and B, first determine the desired **finished** size for the Flying Geese Units. A finished Flying Geese Unit is twice as wide as it is tall. For example, let's use the finished size of 6" w x 3" h.

3. The cutting size for the square A's is the finished width measurement + 1¼". For our example, it would be 6" + 1¼" = 7¼". The cutting size for square A would be 7¼" x 7¼".

4. The cutting size for the square B's is the finished height measurement + ⅞". For our example, it would be 3" + ⅞" = 3⅞". The cutting size for the 4 square B's would be 3⅞" x 3⅞".

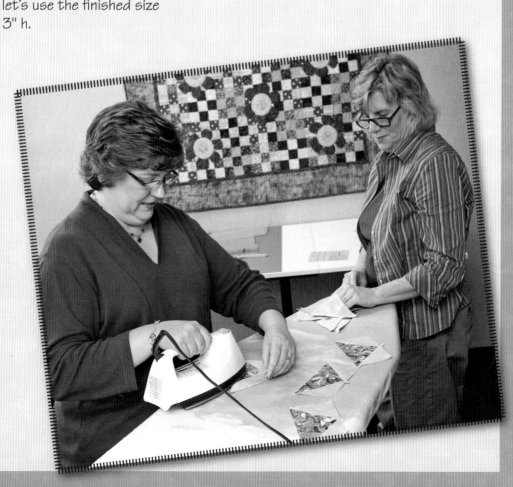

LESSON TWO

In this lesson you will learn about **Setting Blocks on Point**, page 15. In this type of setting the blocks are sewn together in diagonal rows instead of in the more traditional horizontal or vertical rows.

Get to the *Point*

For my Get to the Point quilt, I chose a simple block pattern and alternated the pieced blocks with plain setting squares, which made this quilt fast and easy to piece. The large-scale prints in bold shades of green give this quilt a coordinated decorator look.

Finished Quilt Size: 52" x 69" (132 cm x 175 cm)
Finished Block Size: 12" x 12" (30 cm x 30 cm)

FABRIC REQUIREMENTS

Yardage is based on 43"/44" (109 cm/112 cm) wide fabric.

2¼ yds (2.1 m) of green large floral print
½ yd (46 cm) of green dot print
⅝ yd (57 cm) of green/rust floral print
⅞ yd (80 cm) of dark green floral print (includes binding)
¼ yd (23 cm) of green stripe
½ yd (46 cm) of cream print
4⅜ yds (4 m) of backing fabric

You will also need:

60" x 77" (152 cm x 196 cm) rectangle of batting

CUTTING OUT THE PIECES

Follow **Rotary Cutting**, page 54, to cut fabric. Cut all strips from the selvage-to-selvage width of the fabric. All measurements include ¼" seam allowances.

From green large floral print:

- Cut 2 strips 12½" wide. From these strips, cut 6 **large squares** 12½" x 12½".
- Cut 3 squares 18¾" x 18¾". Cut each square **twice** diagonally to make 12 **side triangles**. (You will use 10 triangles and have 2 remaining.)
- Cut 2 squares 9¾" x 9¾". Cut each square **once** diagonally to make 4 **corner triangles**.

From green dot print:

- Cut 6 strips 2½" wide. From these strips, cut 24 **sashing strips** 2½" x 8½".

From green/rust floral print:

- Cut 2 strips 8½" wide. From these strips, cut 6 **medium squares** 8½" x 8½".

From dark green floral print:

- Cut 2 strips 8½" wide. From these strips, cut 6 **medium squares** 8½" x 8½".
- Cut 7 **binding strips** 1½" wide.

From green stripe:

- Cut 3 strips 2½" wide. From these strips, cut 48 **small squares** 2½" x 2½".

From cream print:

- Cut 6 strips 2½" wide. From these strips, cut 24 **sashing strips** 2½" x 8½".

ASSEMBLING THE BLOCKS

Follow **Piecing**, page 54, and **Pressing**, page 55, to assemble the blocks. Use ¼" seam allowances throughout.

1. Sew 1 green dot print **sashing strip** to opposite sides of 1 dark green floral print **medium square** to make **Unit 1**. Make 6 Unit 1's.

Unit 1 (make 6)

2. Sew 1 **small square** to each end of remaining green dot print **sashing strips** to make **Unit 2**. Make 12 Unit 2's.

Unit 2 (make 12)

3. Sew 1 Unit 2 to opposite sides of Unit 1 to make **Block A**. Make 6 Block A's.

Block A (make 6)

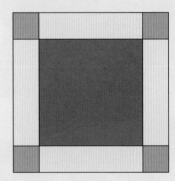

4. Repeat Steps 1-3 using cream print **sashing strips**, green/rust floral print **medium squares**, and **small squares** to make **Block B**. Make 6 Block B's.

Block B (make 6)

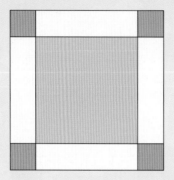

ASSEMBLING THE QUILT TOP

1. Refer to **Setting Blocks on Point**, page 15, to make the quilt top.

FINISHING THE QUILT

1. Follow **Quilting**, page 55, to mark, layer, and quilt. My quilt is quilted with scallops in each sashing strip and large flowers and leaves across the remainder of the quilt.
2. Refer to **Making a Hanging Sleeve**, page 58, to make and attach a hanging sleeve, if desired.
3. Use **binding strips** and follow **Pat's Machine-Sewn Binding**, page 58, to bind quilt.

Setting Blocks on Point

When sewing blocks together in diagonal rows, you will use **Setting Triangles** at the ends of the rows and **Corner Triangles** on the corners to square up the quilt top. **Note:** In the project instructions I had you "over-cut" these triangles so they may appear to be too large when laying out your quilt top. They will be trimmed to the correct size as you sew the quilt top together.

1. Arrange **Block A's, B's, large squares**, and **setting triangles** into diagonal rows. Align bottom edges of setting triangles with bottom edges of blocks for Rows 1-3 (**Fig. 1**). Align top edges of setting triangles with top edges of blocks for Rows 4-6 (**Fig. 2**).

Fig. 1

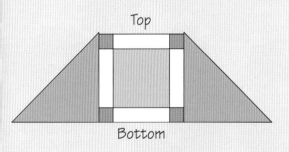

Fig. 2

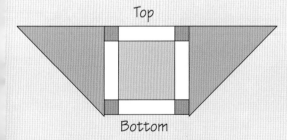

2. Sew Row 1 together. Repeat to sew each remaining row together.

3. Trim the "dog ears" which extend from the setting triangles even with the edges of the blocks (**Fig. 3**).

Fig. 3

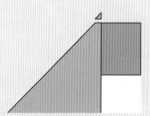

4. Working from top left to bottom right, sew Rows 1-3 together to make the top half of the quilt top (**Fig. 4**). Repeat with Rows 4-6 to make bottom half of the quilt top.

Fig. 4

5. Sew the 2 quilt top sections together with a center seam (**Fig. 5**). Trim the "dog ears" which extend at the corners.

Fig. 5

6. Sew 1 **corner triangle** to each corner to complete **quilt top**.

7. Being careful to keep a 90° angle at the corners and allowing a ¼" seam allowance (**Fig. 6**), square up quilt top by trimming outer edges of setting and corner triangles. **Note:** For this quilt, I chose to leave a larger seam allowance (approximately ½"w). That way, when I add binding, the points of the blocks do not touch the binding and appear to "float".

Fig. 6

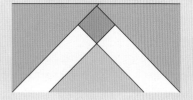

DOING THE MATH

The cutting sizes given in my project instructions include over-cutting the setting and corner triangles. If you would like to calculate cutting sizes for setting and corner triangles for future projects, follow the steps below.

To determine size of side setting triangles:

1. Multiply the finished length of 1 side of the block by 1.414 to determine the diagonal measurement of the block when turned on point. Round up to the nearest 1/8". For example, a 12" finished block would have a diagonal of 16.968 rounded to 17".

2. Add 1 1/4" to this measurement. You would need to cut your squares 18 1/4" x 18 1/4". Cut squares **twice** diagonally. *Note: If you would like your blocks to "float" as my blocks do, add 1 3/4" to the diagonal measurement and cut your squares 18 3/4" x 18 3/4".*

To determine size of corner setting triangles:

1. Multiply the finished length of 1 side of the block by 0.707 to determine the length of the short side of the corner setting triangle. Round up to the nearest 1/8". For example, for a 12" finished block the length of the short side of the corner setting triangle would be 8.484 rounded to 8 1/2".

2. Add 7/8" to this measurement. You would need to cut your squares 9 3/8" x 9 3/8". Cut squares **once** diagonally. *Note: If you would like your blocks to "float" as my blocks do, add 1 1/4" to the determined measurement and cut your squares 9 3/4" x 9 3/4".*

17

LESSON THREE

In this lesson you will be introduced to my easy and accurate technique for Making Triangle-Squares, page 26. You will learn about Chain Piecing, page 29, and how it speeds the piecing process. I also share some handy tips for Sewing Perfect Seam Intersections, page 31. In addition, Crossroads provides you with an opportunity to practice the skills you have learned in previous lessons such as Quick and Easy Flying Geese, page 6, and Setting Blocks on Point, page 15.

Cross Roads

I have always loved this block because it has such strong design. To make an even bolder statement, I chose to use high contrast shades of green and brown from my Sweetbriar II fabric collection from P&B Textiles.

Finished Quilt Size: 89" x 89" (226 cm x 226 cm)
Finished Block Size: 21¹/₄" x 21¹/₄" (54 cm x 54 cm)

FABRIC REQUIREMENTS
Yardage is based on 43"/44" (109 cm/112 cm) wide fabric.
- 2⁵/₈ yds (2.4 m) of green print #1
- 3⁵/₈ yds (3.3 m) of green print #2
- 1³/₈ yds (1.3 m) of brown print #1
- 3¹/₂ yds (3.2 m) of brown print #2 (includes binding)
- 8 yds (7.3 m) of backing fabric

You will also need:
- 96" x 96" (244 cm x 244 cm) square of batting

CUTTING OUT THE PIECES

*Follow **Rotary Cutting**, page 54, to cut fabric. Cut all strips from the selvage-to-selvage width of the fabric. All measurements include ¹/₄" seam allowances.*

From green print #1:
- Cut 2 strips 13¹/₈" wide. From these strips, cut 5 squares 13¹/₈" x 13¹/₈". Cut each square **twice** diagonally to make 20 **setting triangles**.
- Cut 2 strips 6¹/₄" wide. From these strips, cut 10 squares 6¹/₄" x 6¹/₄". Cut each square **once** diagonally to make 20 **corner triangles**.
- Cut 7 strips 3¹/₂" wide. From these strips, cut 20 **strips** 3¹/₂" x 10¹/₂".
- Cut 7 strips 3" wide*. From these strips, cut 80 **small squares** 3" x 3".

From green print #2:
- Cut 2 lengthwise **medium border rectangles** 9¹/₂" x 34¹/₄".
- Cut 2 lengthwise **large border rectangles** 9¹/₂" x 43¹/₄".
- Cut 2 **side middle borders** 2" x 67¹/₄", pieced as needed.
- Cut 2 **top/bottom middle borders** 2" x 70¹/₄", pieced as needed.
- Cut 4 **small border rectangles** 3¹/₂" x 36¹/₂".
- Cut 1 strip 9¹/₂" wide. From this strip, cut 2 **corner border squares** 9¹/₂" x 9¹/₂".
- Cut 5 strips 3⁷/₈" wide. From these strips, cut 48 **large squares** 3⁷/₈" x 3⁷/₈".
- Cut 5 strips 3" wide*. From these strips, cut 64 **small squares** 3" x 3".
- Cut 1 strip 2¹/₂" wide. From this strip, cut 16 **smallest squares** 2¹/₂" x 2¹/₂".
- Cut 1 strip 3¹/₂" wide. From this strip, cut 4 **medium squares** 3¹/₂" x 3¹/₂".

From brown print #1:
- Cut 7 strips 3" wide*. From these strips, cut 80 **small squares** 3" x 3".
- Cut 2 strips 2¹/₂" wide. From these strips, cut 20 **smallest squares** 2¹/₂" x 2¹/₂".
- Cut 1 strip 3¹/₂" wide. From this strip, cut 5 **medium squares** 3¹/₂" x 3¹/₂".
- Cut 10 **binding strips** 1¹/₂" wide.

From brown print #2:
- Cut 2 **side inner borders** 2" x 64¹/₄", pieced as needed.
- Cut 2 **top/bottom inner borders** 2" x 67¹/₄", pieced as needed.
- Cut 3 strips 7¹/₄" wide. From these strips, cut 12 **largest squares** 7¹/₄" x 7¹/₄".
- Cut 2 strips 13¹/₈" wide. From these strips, cut 4 squares 13¹/₈" x 13¹/₈". Cut each square **twice** diagonally to make 16 **setting triangles**.
- Cut 2 strips 6¹/₄" wide. From these strips, cut 8 squares 6¹/₄" x 6¹/₄". Cut each square **once** diagonally to make 16 **corner triangles**.
- Cut 6 strips 3¹/₂" wide. From these strips, cut 16 **strips** 3¹/₂" x 10¹/₂".
- Cut 5 strips 3" wide*. From these strips, cut 64 **small squares** 3" x 3".

* Cutting sizes for small squares are larger than needed to allow for trimming the finished Triangle-Squares as described in **Making Triangle-Squares**, page 26. If you wish to cut your squares to the exact size and not trim, cut your strips 2⁷/₈" wide and then cut the squares 2⁷/₈" x 2⁷/₈".

ASSEMBLING THE BLOCKS
*Follow **Making Triangle-Squares**, page 26, **Chain Piecing**, page 29, **Sewing Perfect Seam Intersections**, page 31, **Piecing**, page 54, and **Pressing**, page 55, to assemble the blocks. Use ¼" seam allowances throughout.*

Triangle-Squares
1. Using green print #1 and brown print #1 **small squares**, make 160 **Triangle-Square A's**. Trim the Triangle-Squares to 2½" x 2½".

Triangle-Square A (make 160)

2. Repeat **Step 1** using green print #2 and brown print #2 **small squares** to make 128 **Triangle-Square B's**.

Triangle-Square B (make 128)

Block A
1. Sew 4 **Triangle-Square A's** together to make **Unit 1**. Make 20 Unit 1's.

Unit 1 (make 20)

2. Sew 4 **Triangle-Square A's** together to make **Unit 2**. Make 20 Unit 2's.

Unit 2 (make 20)

3. Sew 1 brown print #1 **smallest square** to Unit 1 to make **Unit 3**. Make 10 Unit 3's.

Unit 3 (make 10)

4. Sew 1 brown print #1 **smallest square** to Unit 2 to make **Unit 4**. Make 10 Unit 4's.

Unit 4 (make 10)

5. Sew 1 **Unit 3**, 1 **Unit 4**, and 1 green print #1 **strip** together to make **Unit 5**. Make 10 Unit 5's.

Unit 5 (make 10)

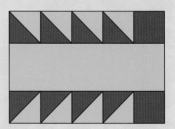

6. Align 1 short edge of 1 green print #1 **setting triangle** with 1 long edge of 1 **Unit 1**. Sew Unit 1 and setting triangle together to make **Unit 6**. Make 10 Unit 6's. Trim the "dog ears" which extend from the setting triangles.

Unit 6 (make 10)

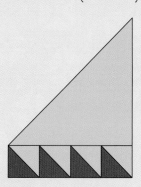

7. Repeat Step 6 to sew 1 **Unit 2** and 1 green print #1 **setting triangle** together to make **Unit 7**. Make 10 Unit 7's.

Unit 7 (make 10)

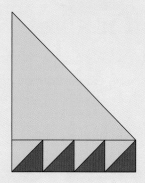

8. Sew 1 **Unit 5**, 1 **Unit 6**, and 1 **Unit 7** together to make **Unit 8**. Make 10 Unit 8's. Trim the "dog ears" which extend from the setting triangles.

Unit 8 (make 10)

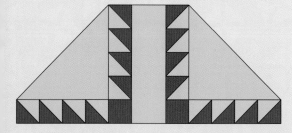

9. Sew 1 brown #1 print **medium square** and 2 green print #1 **strips** together to make **Unit 9**. Make 5 Unit 9's.

Unit 9 (make 5)

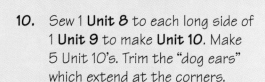

10. Sew 1 **Unit 8** to each long side of 1 **Unit 9** to make **Unit 10**. Make 5 Unit 10's. Trim the "dog ears" which extend at the corners.

Unit 10 (make 5)

11. Sew 1 green print #1 **corner triangle** to each corner of **Unit 10** to make **Block A**. Make 5 Block A's.

Block A (make 5)

12. Centering design and leaving a 1/4" seam allowance on all sides, square blocks to 21³/₄" x 21³/₄".

Block B

1. Repeat **Block A**, Steps 1-12, using **Triangle-Square B's**, brown print #2 **strips**, **setting triangles**, and **corner triangles**, and green print #2 **smallest squares** and **medium squares** to make 4 Block B's.

Block B (make 4)

ASSEMBLING THE QUILT TOP

Refer to ***Quilt Top Diagram*** *for placement.*

1. Sew 2 **Block A's** and 1 **Block B** together to make **Row A**. Make 2 Row A's.
2. Sew 2 **Block B's** and 1 **Block A** together to make **Row B**.
3. Sew **Row A's** and **Row B** together to make **quilt top center**.
4. Sew brown print #2 **side inner borders** to quilt top center.
5. Sew brown print #2 **top/bottom inner borders** to quilt top center.
6. Repeat **Steps 4-5** with green print #2 **middle borders**.

Outer Borders

1. Refer to **Quick and Easy Flying Geese**, page 6, to make 48 Flying Geese Units using green print #2 **large squares** and brown print #2 **largest squares**.

Flying Geese Unit (make 48)

2. Sew 12 **Flying Geese Units** together to make **Unit 11**. Make 4 Unit 11's.

Unit 11 (make 4)

3. Sew 1 **small border rectangle** to each **Unit 11** to make **Unit 12**. Make 4 Unit 12's.

Unit 12 (make 4)

4. Sew 1 **Unit 12** to 1 **medium border rectangle** to make **top outer border**. Repeat to make **bottom outer border**.

5. Sew 1 **Unit 12**, 1 **large border rectangle**, and 1 **corner border square** together to make **side outer border**. Make 2 side outer borders.

6. Sew **top and bottom outer borders** to quilt top.

7. Sew 1 **side outer border** to each side of quilt top.

FINISHING THE QUILT

1. Follow **Quilting**, page 55, to mark, layer, and quilt. My quilt is quilted with outline quilting around the Flying Geese and freeform vines and leaves in the outer border. Block A's have outline quilting in the green Triangle-Squares and freeform vines and leaves in the setting triangles. Block B's have outline quilting in the brown Triangle-Squares and freeform vines and leaves in the setting triangles.

2. Refer to **Making a Hanging Sleeve**, page 58, to make and attach a hanging sleeve, if desired.

3. Use **binding strips** and follow **Pat's Machine-Sewn Binding**, page 58, to bind quilt.

Quilt Top Diagram

MAKING TRIANGLE-SQUARES

I like to over-cut my squares when making Triangle-Squares and then trim them to the correct size after sewing. This insures that my Triangle-Squares will always be exactly the right size. The cutting size given in the project instructions will make Triangle-Squares that are larger than needed and the instructions will tell you the size to trim the Triangle-Squares before assembling the Block or Quilt Top.

1. Draw a diagonal line on wrong side of each lighter-colored square called for in your project instructions (**Fig. 1**).

2. With right sides together, place 1 marked square on top of 1 unmarked square; pin if desired (**Fig. 2**).

Fig. 1

Fig. 2

Note: I used a high contrast thread for photography purposes only. You will want to use a matching or blending thread when making your project.

3. Stitch seam ¼" from each side of drawn line (**Figs. 3-4**).

4. Cut along drawn line (**Figs. 5-6**). Open and press seam allowances toward darker fabric to make 2 **Triangle-Squares** (**Figs. 7-8**).

Fig. 3

Fig. 4

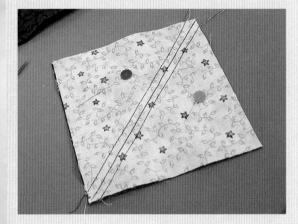

Fig. 5

Fig. 6

Fig. 7

Fig. 8

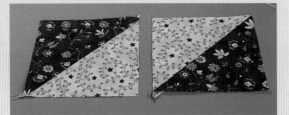

5. Referring to **Fig. 9**, align the 45° angle line on ruler with seamline on Triangle-Square. Trimming as little fabric as possible, trim two adjacent sides of Triangle-Square. Rotate Triangle-Square 180°. Align trimmed edges with desired measurement marks on ruler and trim remaining adjacent sides.

Fig. 9

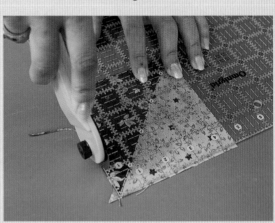

Tip: You can **Chain Piece**, page 29, Triangle-Squares by sewing the 1/4" seam line on one side of the drawn line on all the squares and then turning the chain around and sewing the second seam line.

CHAIN PIECING

To speed the sewing of multiple quilt pieces I like to use Chain Piecing. This technique allows you to sew many pieces together in one continuous chain without cutting the thread between pieces. It's kind of like piecing on an assembly line. Because you only pause briefly between pieces, Chain Piecing will help your work go faster and will usually result in more accurate piecing.

Below I demonstrate Chain Piecing using fabric squares, but Chain Piecing can be used any time you have lots of pieces to sew. It's great for pieces of any shape or size!

Note: I used a high contrast thread for photography purposes only. You will want to use a matching or blending thread when making your project.

1. Matching right sides, place 2 contrasting squares together. Repeat to stack the remaining squares in pairs beside your machine in a position that will allow you to easily pick them up.

2. Sew the first pair together along 1 edge, pausing with needle down just before completing the seam. Without lifting the presser foot and leaving a small space between the pairs of squares, place the next pair under the tip of the presser foot. Finish sewing the seam on the first pair and continue stitching onto the second pair (**Fig. 1**). There will be a thread chain between the pairs (**Fig. 2**).

Fig. 1

Fig. 2

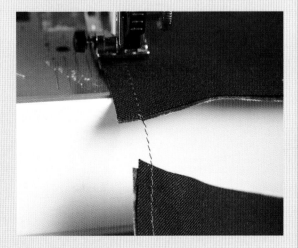

3. Feed the third pair under the presser foot and continue stitching (**Fig. 3**). You are now chain piecing!

Fig. 3

4. Continue chain piecing until you have sewn all of your stacked pairs. Cut the thread chains between the pairs (**Fig. 4**).

Fig. 4

5. Open and press seam allowances toward the darker fabric (**Fig. 5**).

Fig. 5

6. Using Chain Piecing, pieces can be sewn together to make Units and then the Units can be Chain Pieced together to make larger Units (**Fig. 6**).

Fig. 6

SEWING PERFECT
SEAM INTERSECTIONS

- -

Careful matching and stitching across seam allowances when piecing will result in perfectly matched seam intersections.

1. Matching right sides, raw edges, and seams, place 2 units together (**Fig. 1**).

    Fig. 1

    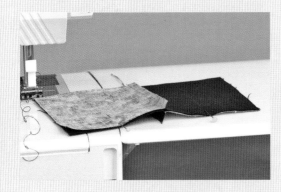

2. Place Unit under the presser foot with the top seam allowance facing the needle (**Fig. 2**). When you sew over this seam, the presser foot will slightly push the seam, butting it snugly against the one below.

    Fig. 2

> **TIP:** Seam allowances must be pressed in opposite directions to butt up properly against each other. If you have consistently pressed toward the darker fabric, your seam allowances will *almost* always line up correctly.

> **Tip:** You may find it helpful to pin pieces in place, removing pins just *before* you are about to sew over them.

LESSON FOUR

In the fourth lesson you will learn about **Paper-Piecing**, page 38. With this technique, your fabric pieces are sewn onto a paper pattern. Also known as Foundation Piecing, this type of piecing has been around for generations. Today, unlike our ancestors who had to draw each pattern by hand, we can easily reproduce multiple copies of a pattern using a copier or printer.

Turkey *Tracks*

I have a collection of 1930's reproduction prints, which I just adore. When I use them, I feel a connection to the women of the '30's that made scrap quilts (some paper-pieced) from feed sacks. For this quilt, I chose lots of my '30's prints but limited my color palette to three colors for a scrappy yet controlled look. For the border I used a Scottie dog print—one of my favorites!

Finished Quilt Size: 47¼" x 47¼" (120 cm x 120 cm)
Finished Block Size: 15¼" x 15¼" (39 cm x 39 cm)

FABRIC REQUIREMENTS

Yardage is based on 43"/44" (109 cm/112 cm) wide fabric.

- 5" x 10" (13 cm x 25 cm) rectangle of at least 16 assorted yellow prints
- 4" x 18" (10 cm x 46 cm) rectangle of at least 16 assorted red prints
- 5" x 10" (13 cm x 25 cm) rectangle of at least 6 assorted peach prints
- ⅝ yd (57 cm) of pale yellow solid
- ¼ yd (23 cm) of medium yellow print
- 1⅛ yds (1 m) of red print for border and binding
- 3 yds (2.7 m) of backing fabric

You will also need:

- 52" x 52" (132 cm x 132 cm) square of batting

CUTTING OUT THE PIECES

*Follow **Rotary Cutting**, page 54, to cut fabric. Cut all strips from the selvage-to-selvage width of the fabric. Cutting lengths for outer borders include an extra 4" for "insurance" and will be trimmed after measuring the completed quilt top center. Pieces for paper piecing are large enough to cover appropriate areas and seam allowances. The remaining pieces include 1/4" seam allowances.*

From assorted yellow prints:
- Cut a **total** of 8 **squares** 4¼" x 4¼" for area 1.
- Cut a **total** of 16 squares 4" x 4". Cut each square **once** diagonally to make 32 **triangles** for areas 4 and 5.

From assorted red prints:
- Cut a **total** of 16 squares 4" x 4". Cut each square **once** diagonally to make 32 **triangles** for areas 2 and 3.
- Cut a **total** of 16 **strips** 4" x 12" for area 6.
- Cut a **total** of 13 **sashing squares** 1¾" x 1¾".

From assorted peach prints:
- Cut 8 squares 4¼" x 4¼". Cut each square **once** diagonally to make 16 **triangles** for area 7.

From pale yellow solid:
- Cut 6 strips 1¾" wide. From these strips, cut 12 **long sashing strips** 1¾" x 15¾".
- Cut 4 strips 1¾" wide. From these strips, cut 16 **short sashing strips** 1¾" x 7½".

From medium yellow print:
- Cut 4 **corner squares** 6½" x 6½".

From red print for border:
- Cut 4 **borders** 6½" x 38¾".
- Cut 6 **binding strips** 1½" wide.

MAKING THE BLOCKS

Use 1/4" seam allowances throughout.

1. Follow **Paper-Piecing**, page 38, to make 16 **Paper-Pieced Units**.

Paper-Pieced Unit (make 16)

2. Sew 2 **Paper-Pieced Units** and 1 **short sashing strip** together to make **Unit 1**. Make 8 Unit 1's.

Unit 1 (make 8)

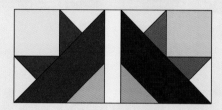

3. Sew 1 **sashing square** and 2 **short sashing strips** together to make **Unit 2**. Make 4 Unit 2's.

Unit 2 (make 4)

4. Sew 2 **Unit 1's** and 1 **Unit 2** together to make a **Turkey Tracks Block**. Make 4 Turkey Tracks Blocks.

Turkey Tracks Block (make 4)

ASSEMBLING THE QUILT TOP CENTER

*Refer to **Quilt Top Diagram** for placement.*

1. Sew 2 **Turkey Tracks Blocks** and 3 **long sashing strips** together to make a **row**. Make 2 rows.

Row (make 2)

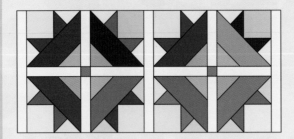

2. Sew 3 **sashing squares** and 2 **long sashing strips** together to make a **sashing row**. Make 3 sashing rows.

Sashing Row (make 3)

3. Sew sashing rows and rows together to make quilt top center.

ADDING THE BORDERS

1. To determine length of **side borders**, measure **length** of quilt top center. Trim 2 borders to determined length.

2. To determine length of **top** and **bottom borders**, measure **width** of quilt top center. Trim remaining borders to determined length.

3. Matching centers and corners, sew side borders to the quilt top center.

4. Sew 1 **corner square** to each end of top and bottom borders.

5. Matching centers and corners, sew top and bottom borders to quilt top.

FINISHING THE QUILT

1. Follow **Quilting**, page 55, to mark, layer, and quilt. My quilt is machine quilted with outline quilting and a wiggly line in the sashings. The red triangles are outline quilted with curved lines. Loops, or "petals," are quilted in the peach triangles and large red areas of each Paper-Pieced Unit, and meandering quilting fills the remainder of the quilt.

2. Refer to **Making a Hanging Sleeve**, page 58, to make and attach a hanging sleeve, if desired.

3. Use **binding strips** and follow **Pat's Machine-Sewn Binding**, page 58, to bind quilt.

Quilt Top Diagram

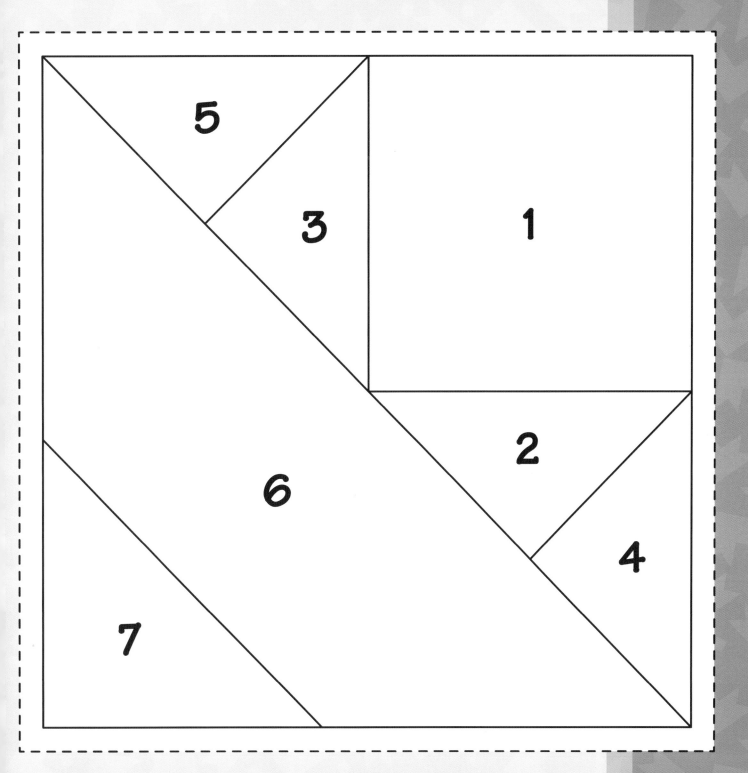

PAPER-PIECING

Because you are actually stitching along printed lines, paper-piecing allows you to piece even the smallest triangles and squares accurately.

Paper-pieced patterns are divided into numbered areas for placement of the fabric pieces. Always begin with 1 and work in numerical order.

Keep in mind that after sewing and pressing open, the pattern and fabric pieces will be wrong sides together.

I demonstrate Paper-Piecing using the fabric pieces from my Turkey Tracks quilt, page 32, but the same steps are used for any paper-piecing project.

> **Tip:** I always make a few extra copies of the paper-piecing pattern. This allows me to make a practice block to get into the flow of the construction. Also, I like to have extras just in case I make a mistake (believe me – it's no fun to "un-sew" paper piecing).

PAPER-PIECING UNITS

1. Photocopy the paper-piecing pattern on page 37, at least 16 times.

> **Very Important:**
> Some photocopied patterns may smear when ironed. Test your patterns to be sure you can iron without transferring ink to your fabric or ironing board. Use a pressing cloth if needed.

2. Use neutral-colored all-purpose thread in needle and bobbin.

> **Very important:**
> Shorten stitch length on sewing machine to 18 stitches per inch (necessary for removal of paper).

3. Place 1 paper-piecing pattern (foundation) onto table with printed side down. Center 1 yellow square, right side up, over area 1 and pin in place (**Fig. 1**). Holding foundation and fabric up to a bright window or other light source, make sure yellow square extends at least ¼" beyond lines of area 1 for seam allowances (**Fig. 2**). Adjust placement of yellow square if needed.

Fig. 1

Fig. 2

4. Choose 2 matching red triangles for areas 2 and 3. With right sides together, align long edge of 1 red triangle with the edge of the yellow square that extends into area 2 (**Fig. 3**). Holding long edge of red triangle, fold triangle over to make sure it will cover all of area 2 (including seam allowances). Hold up to a light as needed to ensure proper placement of red triangle (**Fig. 4**) and pin fabric pieces to foundation (**Fig. 5**).

Fig. 3

Fig. 4

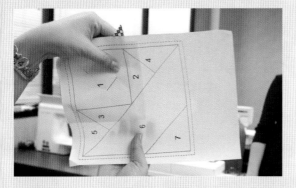

Fig. 5

5. Turn foundation and fabric pieces over so that printed side of foundation is facing up. Beginning at dashed line (edge of seam allowance) on foundation (**Fig. 6**), stitch along line between areas 1 and 2. Stitch line, ending 2 or 3 stitches into the opposite seam allowance (**Fig. 7**).

Fig. 6

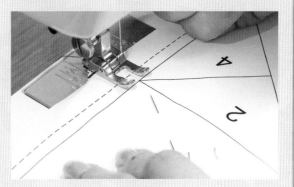

Fig. 7

39

6. Trim seam allowances to ¼" (**Fig. 8**). Open out fabrics and press. Make sure fabrics cover areas, including the ¼" seam allowances.

Fig. 8

Tip: If your fabric does not cover an area, remove seam. Tape over seamline with clear tape, if needed, and stitch seam again. There is no "fix it later" with paper-piecing.

---

7. Continuing in the same manner and using red triangle for area 3, align long edge of triangle with the edge of yellow square that extends into area 3. Holding long edge of red triangle, fold triangle over to make sure it will cover all of area 3 (including seam allowances). Hold up to a light as needed to ensure proper placement of red triangle and pin fabric pieces to foundation.

8. Turn foundation and fabric pieces over so that printed side of foundation is facing up. Beginning at dashed line (edge of seam allowance) on foundation, stitch along line between areas 1 and 3. Stitch line, ending 2 or 3 stitches into the opposite seam allowance.

9. Trim seam allowances to ¼" and press fabric pieces open (**Fig. 9**).

Fig. 9

10. Continue to add each fabric piece to foundation in numeric order, trimming each seam allowance and pressing fabrics open after stitching each seam (**Figs. 10-12**).

Fig. 10

Fig. 11

Fig. 12

11. Using ruler and rotary cutter, trim foundation and fabric pieces along outer dashed line of foundation (**Figs. 13 and 14**).

Fig. 13

Fig. 14

12. Carefully remove paper foundation (**Fig. 15**) to complete **Paper-Pieced Unit**. **Note:** It may be helpful to fold and crease paper along stitched lines (**Fig. 16**).

Paper-Pieced Unit

Fig. 15

Fig. 16

Tip: Paper really dulls sewing machine needles. Be sure to put a new needle in your machine when you are finished paper-piecing.

SUB-CUTTING FABRIC PIECES

Sub-cutting pieces of fabric for paper piecing not only saves time, but it usually saves fabric too. For the Turkey Tracks quilt I gave you the measurements for sub-cutting the pieces, but here's how to determine the sizes to sub-cut your pieces for a future paper-pieced project.

- Place a photocopy of the paper-piecing pattern on a flat surface. Use your ruler to determine how big to sub-cut each piece (**Fig. 1**). Add at least ½" to each side of each area to make sure you have adequate fabric to cover seam allowances and to give yourself a little "wiggle room" in case the fabric slides a little while sewing or you misalign the fabric edges.

Fig. 1

- For odd-shaped areas, such as area 6 on my Turkey Tracks pattern, add ½" along the short sides, but add a little more (an inch or so) to the long sides (**Fig. 2**) to make sure you have adequate fabric to cover those long pointy corners.

Fig. 2

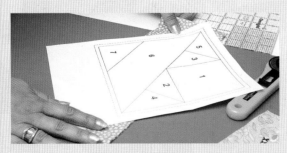

- After cutting the first piece for each area, I like to turn the pattern and fabric piece over and double check my cut (**Fig. 3**). At this point, it's smart to sew a test block and then cut as many pieces as needed for all of the blocks.

Fig. 3

LESSON FIVE

In this lesson I teach the ins and outs of **Easy Curved Cutting and Sewing**, page 49. While this quilt may appear to be difficult at first glance, with careful cutting and piecing you will have the hang of curves in no time flat!

Lover's *Knot*

I thought this would be a great way to use Charm Packs — those pre-cut squares that fabric companies package together. Charm Packs feature all the fabrics in a particular line. But you can use lots of assorted prints from your scrap bag for the same look.

Finished Quilt Size: 51" x 51" (130 cm x 130 cm)
Finished Block Size: 12" x 12" (30 cm x 30 cm)

FABRIC REQUIREMENTS
Yardage is based on 43"/44" (109 cm/112 cm) wide fabric.
   54 charm squares 5" x 5" (13 cm x 13 cm) **or** 1¼ yds
     (1.1 m) **total** of assorted print fabrics
   1½ yds (1.4 m) of blue print
   1⅝ yds* (1.5 m) of yellow floral print
   ½ yd (46 cm) of brown print (includes binding)
   3⅛ yds (2.9 m) of backing fabric
- **You will also need:**
   55" x 55" (140 cm x 140 cm) square of batting

* I used a directional print fabric for my borders. If you use a non-directional fabric and cut all four borders crosswise you will only need ⅞ yd (80 cm) of fabric.

CUTTING OUT THE PIECES

Refer to **Easy Curved Cutting**, page 49, to cut block pieces. Follow **Rotary Cutting**, page 54, to cut remaining pieces. Cut all strips from the selvage-to-selvage width of the fabric. All measurements include $1/4$" seam allowances.

From 5" x 5" charm squares or assorted print fabrics*:

- Cut 36 of **template A**.
- Cut 18 of **template B**.
- Cut 36 **squares** 2" x 2".

From blue print:

- Cut 2 strips 2" wide. From these strips, cut 36 **squares** 2" x 2".
- Cut 1 strip $6^1/2$" wide. From this strip, cut 4 **corner squares** $6^1/2$" x $6^1/2$".
- Cut 5 strips 5" wide. From these strips, cut 36 of **template A**.
- Cut 3 strips 4" wide. From these strips, cut 18 of **template B**.

From yellow floral:

- Cut 2 crosswise **top/bottom outer borders** $6^1/2$" x $38^1/2$".
- Cut 2 lengthwise† **side outer borders** $6^1/2$" x $38^1/2$".

From brown print:

- Cut 2 **top/bottom inner borders** $1^1/2$" x $36^1/2$".
- Cut 2 **side inner borders** $1^1/2$" x $38^1/2$".
- Cut 6 **binding strips** $1^1/2$"w.

* If cutting from scraps of assorted print fabrics, cut 5" wide strips for the piece A's and 4" wide strips for the piece B's. Then cut your own 5" charm squares for the piece A's and 4" squares for the piece B's. This makes the cutting go a lot quicker!

† If using a directional print. For non-directional fabric, cut crosswise side outer borders.

ASSEMBLING THE BLOCKS

Follow **Piecing**, page 54, and **Pressing**, page 55, to assemble the blocks. Use $1/4$" seam allowances throughout.

(**Note:** For each block you will need 4 **A's**, 2 **B's**, and 4 **squares** each from blue print and from assorted prints.)

1. Sew 1 blue print **A** and 2 assorted **squares** together to make **Unit 1**. Make 2 Unit 1's.

Unit 1 (make 2)

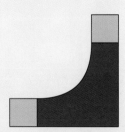

> **Tip:** You can **Chain Piece**, page 29, the squares to the piece A's.

2. Follow **Easy Curved Sewing**, page 51, to sew curved seams. Sew 1 blue print A and 1 assorted B together to make Unit 2. Make 2 Unit 2's.

Unit 2 (make 2)

3. Sew 1 **Unit 1** and 1 **Unit 2** together to make **Unit 3**. Make 2 Unit 3's.

Unit 3 (make 2)

4. Repeat **Steps 1 - 3** using 2 blue print **squares**, 2 assorted **A's**, and 1 blue print **B** to make **Unit 4**. Make 2 Unit 4's.

5. Sew 1 **Unit 3** and 1 **Unit 4** together to make **Unit 5**. Make 2 Unit 5's.

Unit 4 (make 2)

Unit 5 (make 2)

6. Sew 2 **Unit 5's** together to make **Block**.

Block

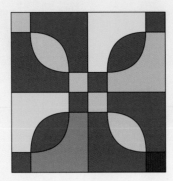

7. Repeat **Steps 1 - 6** to make 9 **blocks**.

ASSEMBLING THE QUILT TOP CENTER

1. Sew 3 blocks together to make a **row**. Make 3 rows.
2. Sew rows together to make **quilt top center**.

ADDING THE BORDERS

1. Sew **top/bottom inner borders** to quilt top center.
2. Sew **side inner borders** to quilt top center.
3. Sew **top/bottom outer borders** to quilt top.
4. Sew 1 **corner square** to each end of each side outer border.
5. Sew **side outer borders** to quilt top.

FINISHING THE QUILT

1. Follow **Quilting**, page 55, to mark, layer, and quilt. My quilt is quilted with a large X through each block. There is a leaf design quilted through each A piece. The inner border is quilted on each side with in the ditch quilting and the outer border is quilted with large leaf patterns.
2. Refer to **Making a Hanging Sleeve**, page 58, to make and attach a hanging sleeve, if desired.
3. Use **binding strips** and follow **Pat's Machine-Sewn Binding**, page 58, to bind quilt.

Quilt Top Diagram

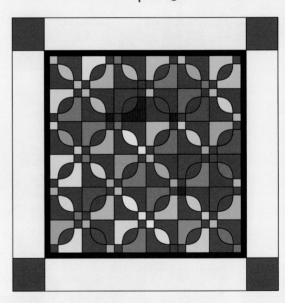

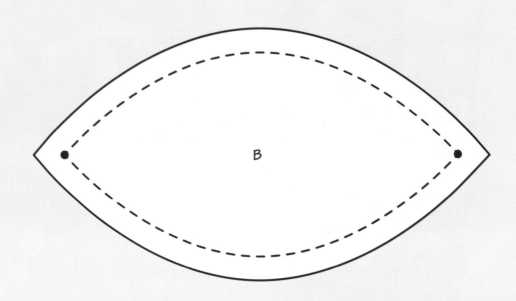

B

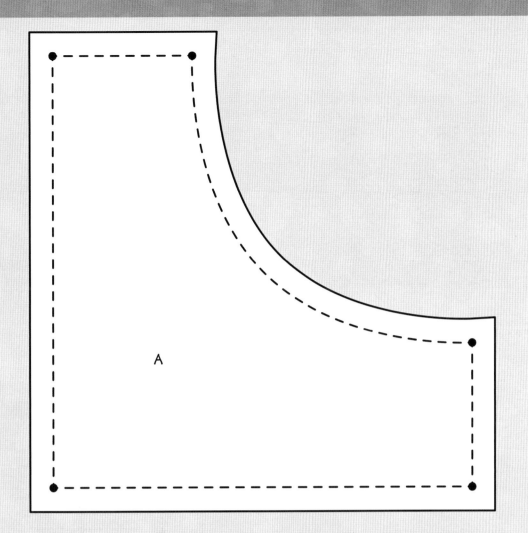

A

EASY CURVED CUTTING

1. Trace patterns, A and B, onto paper (or make photocopies). Cut out patterns.

2. Aligning the pattern with sides of the charm square, cut piece A (**Figs. 1-2**).

Fig. 2

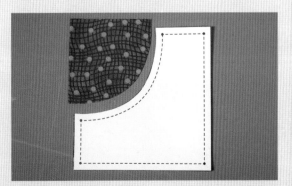

Fig. 1

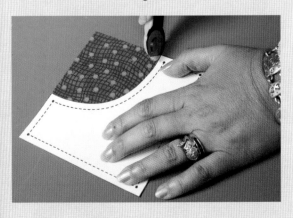

Tip: Yes, I cut these curves with a rotary cutter! I use a nice **new**, **sharp** rotary cutter and I go **very slowly** around the curves. A small revolving cutting mat is also very helpful. It allows me to turn the fabric without lifting it to cut the sides of each piece.

3. Cut a 2" square from the remaining piece (**Fig. 3**).

Fig. 3

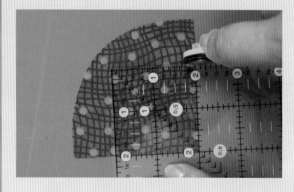

4. Laying the pattern at an angle across the corner of the charm square, cut piece B (**Figs. 4-5**).

Fig. 4

Fig. 5

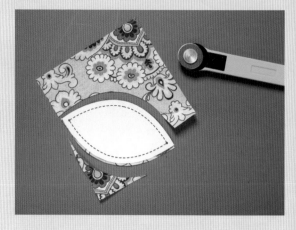

5. Cut a 2" square from the remaining piece (**Fig. 6**).

Fig. 6

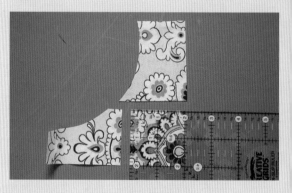

Tip: Cut all the shapes out first, stacking them in piles. Then have fun mixing and matching the pieces to make up the blocks.

Tip: Cut a few extra blocks just in case you want to practice sewing curved seams before you begin working on your quilt.

EASY CURVED SEWING

Tip: I like to think of the tapered piece (piece B) as a melon shape. When sewing curved seams, I like to use the **MOB method** – melons on bottom all the time. I **always** place the piece B on the bottom when sewing the curved seam.

Fig. 3

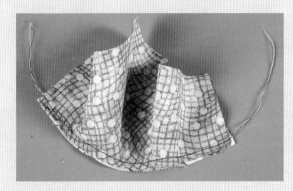

1. Matching right sides, use 2 pins to pin 1 piece A and 1 piece B together at each end. With B on the bottom and keeping raw edges together, slowly sew seam (**Figs. 1-3**) to make Unit 2.

Tip: Using a stiletto to hold the raw edges together while sewing can be very helpful.

Fig. 1

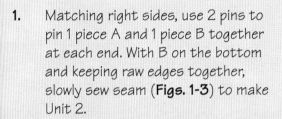

Tip: When sewing curved seams, use the needle down feature on your sewing machine.

Fig. 2

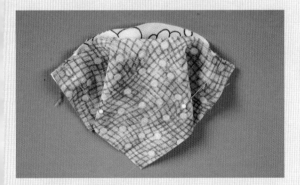

Tip: **GO SLOW** to start. Once you get in the groove of sewing it will be easy... **trust me**!

2. Press seam allowances toward A (**Fig. 4**).

Fig. 4

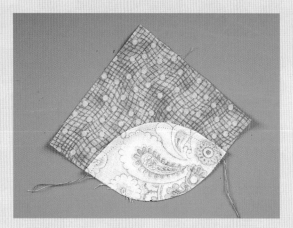

3. Matching right sides, use 2 pins to pin a Unit 1 and a Unit 2 together at each end. With Unit 2 on the bottom and keeping raw edges together, slowly sew seam (**Figs. 5-6**) to make Unit 3.

Fig. 5

Fig. 6

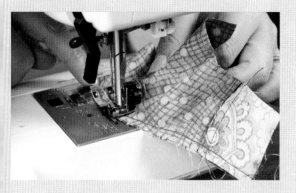

4. Press seam allowances toward Unit 1. Unit 3 should measure 6½" x 6½" (**Figs. 7-8**).

Fig. 8

Fig. 7

GENERAL INSTRUCTIONS

To make your quilting easier and more enjoyable, we encourage you to carefully read all of the general instructions, study the color photographs, and familiarize yourself with the individual project instructions before beginning a project.

ROTARY CUTTING

Rotary cutting has brought speed and accuracy to quiltmaking by allowing quilters to easily cut strips of fabric and then cut those strips into smaller pieces.

- Place fabric on work surface with fold closest to you.

- Square left edge of fabric using rotary cutter and rulers (**Figs. 1 – 2**).

Fig. 1

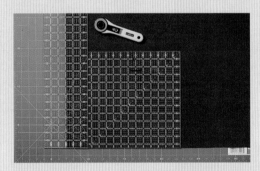

Fig. 2

- Cut all strips from the selvage-to-selvage width of the fabric unless otherwise indicated in project instructions.

- To cut each strip required for a project, place ruler over cut edge of fabric, aligning desired marking on ruler with cut edge; make cut (**Fig. 3**).

Fig. 3

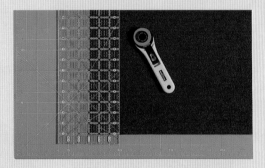

- When cutting several strips from a single piece of fabric, it is important to make sure that cuts remain at a perfect right angle to the fold; square fabric as needed.

PIECING

Precise cutting, followed by accurate piecing, will ensure that all pieces of quilt top fit together well.

- Set sewing machine stitch length for approximately 11 stitches per inch.

- Use neutral-colored general-purpose sewing thread (not quilting thread) in needle and in bobbin.

- An accurate 1/4" seam allowance is essential. Presser feet that are 1/4" wide are available for most sewing machines.

- When piecing, always place pieces right sides together and match raw edges; pin if necessary.

- Chain Piecing, page 29, saves time and will usually result in more accurate piecing.

- Trim away points of seam allowances that extend beyond edges of sewn pieces.

PRESSING

- Use steam iron set on "Cotton" for all pressing.

- Press after sewing each seam.

- Seam allowances are almost always pressed to one side, usually toward darker fabric. However, to reduce bulk it may occasionally be necessary to press seam allowances toward the lighter fabric or even to press them open.

- To prevent dark fabric seam allowance from showing through light fabric, trim darker seam allowance slightly narrower than lighter seam allowance.

- To press long seams, such as those in long strip sets, without curving or other distortion, lay strips across width of the ironing board.

QUILTING

Quilting holds the three layers (top, batting, and backing) of the quilt together and can be done by hand or machine. Because marking, layering, and quilting are interrelated and may be done in different orders depending on circumstances, please read entire **Quilting** section, pages 55 – 58, before beginning project.

TYPES OF QUILTING DESIGNS

In the Ditch Quilting
Quilting along seamlines or along edges of appliquéd pieces is called "in the ditch" quilting. This type of quilting should be done on side **opposite** seam allowance and does not have to be marked.

Outline Quilting
Quilting a consistent distance, usually $1/4$", from seam or appliqué is called "outline" quilting. Outline quilting may be marked, or $1/4$" masking tape may be placed along seamlines for quilting guide. (Do not leave tape on quilt longer than necessary, since it may leave an adhesive residue.)

Motif Quilting
Quilting a design, such as a feathered wreath, is called "motif" quilting. This type of quilting should be marked before basting quilt layers together.

Echo Quilting
Quilting that follows the outline of an appliquéd or pieced design with two or more parallel lines is called "echo" quilting. This type of quilting does not need to be marked.

Channel Quilting
Quilting with straight, parallel lines is called "channel" quilting. This type of quilting may be marked or stitched using a guide.

Crosshatch Quilting
Quilting straight lines in a grid pattern is called "crosshatch" quilting. Lines may be stitched parallel to edges of quilt or stitched diagonally. This type of quilting may be marked or stitched using a guide.

Meandering Quilting
Quilting in random curved lines and swirls is called "meandering" quilting. Quilting lines should not cross or touch each other. This type of quilting does not need to be marked.

Stipple Quilting

Meandering quilting that is very closely spaced is called "stipple" quilting. Stippling will flatten the area quilted and is often stitched in background areas to raise appliquéd or pieced designs. This type of quilting does not need to be marked.

MARKING QUILTING LINES

Quilting lines may be marked using fabric marking pencils, chalk markers, water- or air-soluble pens, or lead pencils.

Simple quilting designs may be marked with chalk or chalk pencil after basting. A small area may be marked, and then quilted, before moving to next area to be marked. Intricate designs should be marked before basting using a more durable marker.

Caution: Pressing may permanently set some marks. Test different markers on scrap fabric to find one that marks clearly and can be thoroughly removed.

A wide variety of pre-cut quilting stencils, as well as entire books of quilting patterns, are available. Using a stencil makes it easier to mark intricate or repetitive designs.

To make a stencil from a pattern, center template plastic over pattern and use a permanent marker to trace pattern onto plastic. Use a craft knife with single or double blade to cut channels along traced lines (**Fig. 4**).

Fig. 4

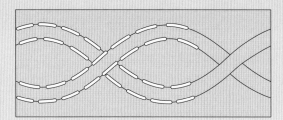

PREPARING THE BACKING

To allow for slight shifting of quilt top during quilting, backing should be approximately 2" to 4" larger on all sides. Yardage requirements listed for quilt backings are calculated for 43"/44"w fabric. Using 90"w or 108"w fabric for the backing of a bed-sized quilt may eliminate piecing. To piece a backing using 43"/44"w fabric, use the following instructions.

1. Measure length and width of quilt top; add 8" (4" for smaller quilts or wall hangings) to each measurement.
2. Cut backing fabric into two lengths slightly longer than determined length measurement. Trim selvages. Place lengths with right sides facing and sew long edges together, forming tube (**Fig. 5**). Match seams and press along one fold (**Fig. 6**). Cut along pressed fold to form single piece (**Fig. 7**).

Fig. 5	Fig. 6	Fig. 7

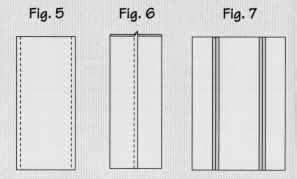

3. Trim backing to size determined in **Step 1**; press seam allowances open.

CHOOSING THE BATTING

The appropriate batting will make quilting easier. For fine hand quilting, choose low-loft batting. All cotton or cotton/polyester blend battings work well for machine quilting because the cotton helps "grip" quilt layers. If quilt is to be tied, a high-loft batting, sometimes called extra-loft or fat batting, may be used to make quilt "fluffy."

Types of batting include cotton, polyester, wool, cotton/polyester blend, cotton/wool blend, and silk.

When selecting batting, refer to package labels for characteristics and care instructions. Cut batting same size as prepared backing.

ASSEMBLING THE QUILT

1. Examine wrong side of quilt top closely; trim any seam allowances and clip any threads that may show through front of the quilt. Press quilt top, being careful not to "set" any marked quilting lines.

2. Place backing wrong side up on flat surface. Use spring clamps or masking tape to secure edges of backing to surface. Place batting on top of backing fabric. Smooth batting gently, being careful not to stretch or tear. Center quilt top right side up on batting.

3. Use 1" rustproof safety pins to "pin-baste" all layers together, spacing pins approximately 4" apart. Begin at center and work toward outer edges to secure all layers. If possible, place pins away from areas that will be quilted, although pins may be removed as needed when quilting.

MACHINE QUILTING METHODS

Straight-Line Quilting

The following instructions are for straight-line quilting, which requires a walking foot or even-feed foot. The term "straight-line" is somewhat deceptive, since curves (especially gentle ones) as well as straight lines can be stitched with this technique.

1. Using the same color general-purpose thread in the needle and bobbin avoids "dots" of bobbin thread being pulled to the surface.

2. Using general-purpose thread, which matches the backing in the bobbin, will add pattern and dimension to the quilt without adding contrasting color. Refer to your owner's manual for recommended tension settings.

3. Set stitch length for 6 to 10 stitches per inch and attach the walking foot to sewing machine.

4. After pin-basting, decide which section of the quilt will have the longest continuous quilting line, oftentimes the area from center top to center bottom. Leaving the area exposed where you will place your first line of quilting, roll up each edge of the quilt to help reduce the bulk, keeping fabrics smooth. Smaller projects may not need to be rolled.

5. Start stitching at beginning of longest quilting line, using very short stitches for the first $1/4$" to "lock" quilting. Stitch across project, using one hand on each side of walking foot to slightly spread fabric and to guide fabric through machine. Lock stitches at end of quilting line.

6. Continue machine quilting, stitching longer quilting lines first to stabilize quilt before moving on to other areas.

Free-Motion Quilting

Free-motion quilting may be free form or may follow a marked pattern.

1. Using the same color general-purpose thread in the needle and bobbin avoids "dots" of bobbin thread being pulled to the surface. Use general-purpose thread in the bobbin and decorative thread for stitching, such as metallic, variegated or contrasting-colored general-purpose thread, when you desire the quilting to be more pronounced.

2. Use a darning foot and lower or cover feed dogs. Pull up bobbin thread and hold both thread ends while you stitch 2 or 3 stitches in place to lock thread. Cut threads near quilt surface.

3. Place hands lightly on quilt on either side of darning foot to slightly spread fabric and to move fabric through the machine. Even stitch length is achieved by using smooth, flowing hand motion and steady machine speed. Slow machine speed and fast hand movement will create long stitches. Fast machine speed and slow hand movement will create short stitches. Move quilt sideways, back and forth, in a circular motion, or in a random motion to create desired designs; do not rotate quilt. Lock stitches at end of each quilting line.

MAKING A HANGING SLEEVE

Attaching a hanging sleeve to back of wall hanging or quilt before the binding is added allows your project to be displayed on a wall.

1. Measure width of quilt top edge and subtract 1". Cut piece of fabric 7"w by determined measurement.
2. Press short edges of fabric piece 1/4" to wrong side; press edges 1/4" to wrong side again and machine stitch in place.
3. Matching wrong sides, fold piece in half lengthwise to form tube.
4. Before sewing binding to quilt, match raw edges and pin hanging sleeve to center top edge on back of quilt.
5. Bind quilt, treating hanging sleeve as part of backing.
6. Blindstitch bottom of hanging sleeve to backing, taking care not to stitch through to front of quilt.

PAT'S MACHINE-SEWN BINDING

For a quick and easy finish when attaching straight-grain binding with overlapped corners, Pat sews her binding to the back of the quilt and Machine Blanket Stitches it in place on the front, eliminating all hand stitching.

1. With right sides together and using diagonal seams (**Fig. 8**), sew the short ends of the binding strips together, if needed, to achieve the necessary length for each edge of quilt.

Fig. 8

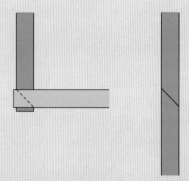

2. Press seam allowances open. Press one long edge of binding 1/4" to the wrong side.
3. Using a narrow zigzag or straight stitch, stitch around quilt close to the raw edges (**Fig. 9**). Trim backing and batting even with edges of quilt top.

Fig. 9

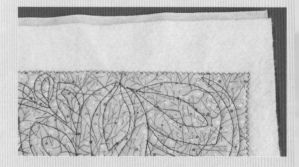

4. Matching raw edges and using a 1/4" seam allowance, sew binding to top and bottom edges on **back** of quilt.

5. Fold binding over to quilt front and pin pressed edges in place, covering stitching line (**Fig. 10**); Blanket Stitch or Top Stitch binding close to pressed edge. Trim ends of top and bottom binding even with edges of quilt top.

Fig. 13

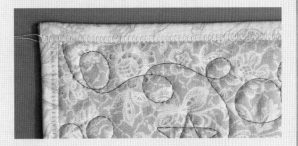

Fig. 10

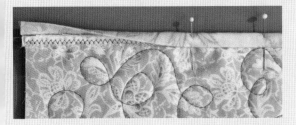

6. Leaving approximately 1½" of binding at each end, stitch a length of binding to **back** of each side of quilt (**Fig. 11**).

Fig. 11

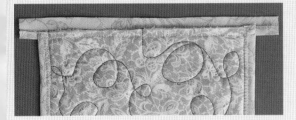

7. Trim each end of binding ½" longer than bound edge. Fold under each raw end of binding (**Fig. 12**); pin in place. Fold binding over to quilt front and Blanket Stitch or Top Stitch in place, (**Fig. 13**).

Fig. 12

SIGNING AND DATING YOUR QUILT

A completed quilt is a work of art and should be signed and dated. There are many different ways to do this and numerous books on the subject. The label should reflect the style of the quilt, the occasion or person for which it was made, and the quilter's own particular talents. Following are some suggestions for recording the history of your quilt or adding a sentiment for future generations.

-   Embroider quilter's name, date, and any additional information on quilt top or backing. Matching floss, such as cream floss on white border, will leave a subtle record. Bright or contrasting floss will make the information stand out.

-   Make label from muslin and use permanent marker to write information. Use different colored permanent markers to make label more decorative. Stitch label to back of quilt.

-   Use photo-transfer paper to add an image to a white or cream fabric label. Stitch label to back of quilt.

-   Piece an extra block from quilt top pattern to use as label. Add information with permanent fabric pen. Appliqué block to back of quilt.

Meet *Pat Sloan*

Want to know anything about quilts? Just ask Pat Sloan. Or attend her workshop. Or get one of her books. Want to stump Pat Sloan? Ask her about her hobbies.

"Well," she says after a long pause and a chuckle, "I like to garden. But really, my life is all about quilting, twenty-four/seven."

"Our time to just relax happens while my husband and I travel for work," the Virginia resident says. "Gregg and I drive to most of our workshops and lectures because of all the quilts and equipment we bring along. We meet the nicest people and get to see lots of new places that are within a day's drive from home.

"I've been fulltime at this career since 2000. Gregg does the management, shipping, ordering, accounting, wrangling the quilts and the sound equipment—keeping me free to teach, lecture, and do the creative side."

And create, she does! Allocating her at-home time between drawing patterns and developing fabrics, Pat still finds time to update her Web site. Visitors to QuiltersHome.com can read her blog, subscribe to her newsletter, and check for workshops in their area. They'll also find a variety of publications, patterns, notions, and Pat's popular fabric lines from P&B Textiles, all available for purchase. There are even a few freebie patterns just for inspiration.

With their business doing so well, you might think that the Sloans would be ready to just sit back and take it easy now and then. Instead, Gregg and Pat have found a way to take their work with them on vacation. They've recently added quilting cruises to their schedule of events, with Pat teaching up to 50 students between ports of call.

In an affectionate salute to their favorite designer, Pat's most devoted fans call themselves "Sloanies." To get a peek into one of the reasons why she's so admired, take a look at her energetic (yet lovely) fabrics, whimsical patterns, and friendly publications: Pat knows that today's quilters want to enjoy themselves while they learn. And if there's anyone who can take the fun craft of quilting and make it downright exhilarating, it's Pat Sloan.